7-Day Emergency Help for OWIAC's

S.O.S. Devotionals

By

E.A. James

FM Publishing Company
Cherokee, NC 28719

7-Day Emergency Help for OWIAC's
S.O.S. Devotionals

Published by:

FM Publishing Company

P.O. Box 215

Cherokee, NC 28719

United States of America

www.fmpublishingcompany.com

Printed in the United States of America

ISBN 9781931671422

Table of Contents

What is OWIAC?

OWIAC stands for "Of Whom I Am Chief." It is pronounced "how we act."

For those of us who are sinners saved by grace through faith, the name fits doesn't it? The apostle Paul made this statement about himself. Like the apostle Paul, we are all sinners saved by grace.

This book contains exactly 7 devotionals for OWIAC's who need emergency help. It is especially helpful during a 7-day fast. Start each morning with your Bible in hand day or night and be prepared to receive healing, enlightenment, peace, and forgiveness from each devotional that ends with a few short, original verses of poetry.

Note that these devotionals use the original Hebraic names for God, Lord, Jehovah, and Jesus Christ. Therefore, the reader will see Yahweh or Yah and Messiah or Yahoshua. Those who are true Bible students will understand and know. However, scripture is quoted exactly as it appears in the King James Version.

This book contains exactly 7 devotionals for OWIAC's who need emergency help. It is especially helpful during a 7-day fast. Start each morning with your Bible in hand day or night and be prepared to receive healing, enlightenment, peace, and forgiveness from each devotional that ends with a few short, original verses of poetry.

Note that these devotionals use the original Hebraic names for God, Lord, Jehovah, and Jesus Christ. Therefore, the reader will see Yahweh or Yah and Messiah or Yahoshua. Those who are true Bible students will understand and know. However, scripture is quoted exactly as it appears in the King James Version.

Day 1: Sunday

A Broken Heart and Contrite Spirit

I shall not be moved. Good scripture to live by, but how do we get to this point? There are times when I think I'm strong, and with certainty, this is when I am liable to fall. A man should never think more highly of himself than he ought to think (Romans 12:3). What a blow and contradiction to those who spout theories about self-esteem. However, our boast in anything comes from our boast in the Creator (Psalm 34:2). We are but "crazy dust" as one of my sisters always says. We are made of mud, yet from the loving and skillful hands of Yahweh. He created us perfect but made us free agents with a free will. Our first parents, Adam and Eve, screwed up. Our Father sent us Messiah Yahoshua as a remedy. However, we have been screwing up ever since. The good news is we can repent, ask for forgiveness, and be assured that the blood sacrifice of our Savior not only covers us but is the propitiation for our sins. It is without a doubt that in these mortal bodies we will sin, we will screw up, and we will fall short of Yah's glory, no matter how hard we try. Therefore, the only conclusion is that we will be judged on just how *hard* we try, how *well* we succeed, and how *committed* we are to the end.

The Book of Revelation tell us that Messiah is soon to return and his reward is with him to give to everyone according to his works (Rev. 22:12), because "faith without works is dead" (James 2:20). However, in another scripture Yahoshua says that not everyone who says to him, "Lord, Lord," will enter into the Kingdom of Heaven, but rather, he that does the will of our Father in Heaven (Matthew 7:21). There is much difference between preachers as to where and what the Kingdom of Heaven is. However, we do know that where the Messiah is, there we will be also, that is, if we make it in by doing the Father's will.

So, what is the Father's will? The Word says that we should love Yahweh and keep his commandments, and that this is the whole duty of man (Ecclesiastes 12:13). Sounds pretty straight forward and to the point, yet at times we believe it's got to be more than that, and other times, we believe it's way too much. Stated simply, our Father wants us to love him and obey him. This is the same thing Yahoshua said when he told his disciples that "if you love me, keep my commandments" (John 14:15). He reiterated what the Father said: "Love the Father with all your heart, soul, and mind" and "Love your neighbor as yourself" (Mark 12:30-31). All of the commandments (Royal Law) were rolled up into these two commandments.

So, what happens when you disobey or do wrong to the person you love? If you are truly sorry for what you have done, you will have a broken heart and a contrite spirit. This means your heart will feel as though it were physically torn, emotionally you will feel remorse, psychologically you will feel anguish, and spiritually you will feel depleted and devoid, needing reconnection and fulfillment. Yahoshua said "blessed are the poor in spirit for theirs is the Kingdom of Heaven" (Matthew 5:3). When you are poor in spirit, you understand and realize your need for the Savior and for the Father. Your soul pants after Yah as the "hart pants after the water brook." (Psalm 42:1)

David knew this better than anyone. Yahweh had delivered him multiple times from the hands of Saul. In the 34th Psalm, verse 18, David said, "The Lord is near unto them that are of a broken heart, and saves such that be of a contrite spirit." After David sinned with Bathsheba and had her husband killed to cover up his sin, he pled his case before the Father. Why? Because David was a man after the Father's own heart. (Acts 13:22) David broke this heart-to-heart connection. It broke his heart because he knew he had broken the Father's heart. David recognized his sin before the Father. He cried out, "Create in me a clean heart, O' God, and renew a right spirit within me." (Psalm 51:10) When you have wronged someone you love and you are remorseful, you want that relationship restored. This caused David to plead with the Father: "Cast me not away from your presence, and take not your holy spirit from me." (Verse 11) David prayed, "Restore unto me the joy of your salvation; and uphold me with your free spirit." (Verse 12)

David learned, as do all sinners, that: "The sacrifices of God are a broken spirit, a broken and contrite heart, O' God, you will not despise." (Psalm 51:17). Sometimes we believe that we need to fast 40 days and 40 nights, give all our substance away so that we have nothing, or even become martyrs. If these things make you feel better or you need them to draw closer to the Father, he honors them; however, he simply asks for our love and obedience. However, when we do sin, and we will no matter how hard we try, we know that we have an advocate with the Father. He says that "if we confess our sins, he is faithful and just to forgive our sins, and cleanse us from all unrighteousness." (1 John 1:9)

It is from this point that we rely on the Father's grace and mercy. The Bible says that, as far as the east is from the west, he forgets our confessed and repented sins. Helen Baylor even recorded a beautiful song about this "sea of forgetfulness." David, too, knew this. In Psalm 62, he conceded that, "Truly my soul waits upon God: from him comes my salvation. He only is my rock and my salvation; he is my defense; I shall not be greatly moved." David even repeated these words in Verse 5 with a slight variation because he also understood that his "expectation is from him" and reiterated his steadfastness in the Father when he said, "I shall not be moved" (Verse 6). Finally, David encouraged all of us sinners to "Trust in him [Yahweh] at all times you people; pour out your heart before him: God is a refuge for us" (Verse

8). So let us always consider what it takes for us to get to this point and continue in this vein.

Day 1 S.O.S. Words of Inspiration

My heart and my spirit lay open before Yah
Is it any wonder that I can cry Halleluyah?

My redeemer lives and I'm saved once more
His grace and mercy have left open the door

Praises, sing praises, with all of my heart
Healed one more time from the enemy's dart

Day 2: Monday

Good Reason to Stop Sinning

Let's face it: sin feels good, if only for a short time. Yes, it is only for a short time. The consequences are longer – much longer. Isn't it a shame we don't consider this before we commit our fun-filled acts?

We go through it every time, no matter what our sin. Deep inside we're depressed, hurt, insecure, and well aware of our mortality and the futility of this life apart from our Creator. These feelings seldom surface in public; after all, we don't want to spoil anyone else's fun. We drink to excess, smoke or snort to excess, and everything else to excess to rid ourselves of any inhibitions. That way, we aren't responsible for our horrible acts. In fact, we usually don't remember what happened – or at least that's what we tell everyone. So, we have our fleeting moments of fun and revel in our sin. That is, until the next morning.

Sometimes we think Yah created mornings as a means of making us pay for our night-filled with sin, or fun as we call it. People loved the movie, Hangover, because they could very well relate to it. However, the consequences are a lot worse. You'd think the sheer absurdity of it all would make us stop. Absolutely not. You'd think the problems we've caused as a result would make us stop. Not usually. Finally, you'd think that little thing Yah put within us that becomes overbearing at times, called our conscience, would cause us to stop. Of course, it hasn't been for lack of trying. We feel terrible when we realize the next day that "Oh hell, not again."

The good news is we do have choices. We can ignore that terrible feeling and that nagging conscience and choose to throw caution to the wind and just do what we feel anytime, anywhere, with anyone, and tell Yah and his fun-stealer to take a hike. This, my friends, is when we know we've taken that one step beyond into the realm of a reprobate mind. And, believe it or not, it's our choice to make.

But, once again, there are those awful consequences that take all the fun out of everything. This time, however, the ultimate consequences are more than just a lost job, spouse, relationship, children, money, peace of mind, physical health, mental stability, and freedom (jail time for DUI). No, my friend, the loss of the above are a piece of cake compared to what Yah has in store for us. Let's take a look.

Oh, no – not more scripture! Well, it's the standard we go by and the only map we have through this temporary wilderness. Someone once held up the Bible and said, "This book will keep me from sin and sin will keep me from this book." Oh, how true his statement was. Of course, we can, due to our freewill, choose to toss it aside or remain ignorant and live in sinful bliss. However, anyone who has ever gotten a traffic ticket for a law they didn't know about, know that "ignorance is no excuse for the law." The same is true for Yah's law.

In the Book of Revelation, Chapter 21, we see a new heaven and new earth created, and the holy city, the holy Jerusalem, is coming down from Heaven. There is no more death, no more tears, no more wars, no sorrow, and no pain. The reason is that "the tabernacle of Yah is with men," he sits upon the throne, and we will be his people and he will be our Yah (Verses 3-5). Our Savior says he is the Alpha and Omega, the beginning and the end, and he will give to him that is "athirst of the fountain of the water of life freely" (Verse 6). Verses 9-26 describe the splendor of this place where immortals will dwell. No sun or moon needed because the glory of Yah and the Lamb are the light. Every kind of precious stone, including the city of gold is there; however, you no longer need money. It describes the walls and gates that represent the 12 tribes of Israel. It is more than what can be described in mere words. Who would want to miss out on all of this? Is it really possible to miss out on it? Won't we all be there?

Everything comes with conditions. There is no such thing as a free lunch. What about Yah's free gift of our Savior to the world? Again, there are conditions that must be met. Either you pay with your money, your time, or with some other intangible commodity like commitment, self-respect, dignity, or conscience. Verse 7 tells us about Yah's conditions with a promise: "He that overcomes shall inherit all things; and I will be his Yah and he shall be my son." Wow, we like the inheriting all things and becoming the sons of Yah; however, that overcoming part cramps our style. However, there's more.

By now we know how Yah works. There are consequences for not choosing the best soul-saving practices. It always comes with a big "BUT" and it's found in Verse 8. See if we can find ourselves in here somewhere, or maybe everywhere:

> "But to the cowards, unbelievers, detestable persons, murderers, the sexually immoral, and those who practice magic spells, idol worshipers, and all those who lie, their place will be in the lake that burns with fire and sulfur. That is the second death."

If ever we needed a reason to stop sinning, here it is folks. I know what it's like to burn my hand; I couldn't imagine undergoing this. Note that it says "the second death." This means we don't escape it by committing suicide. We all will have to stand before a just and Holy Father and give an account for everything we say and do, and yes, for everything we were supposed to do and did not.

Day 2 S.O.S. Words of Inspiration

Oh yes, I reveled in my fun-filled sin
I did this without fail again and again

There were the night seasons of joy
And painful mornings of "Oh, boy!"

Yet I scoffed at the Word and even left it hissing
Until I learned just what I'd be missing

Eternal life with my Father in a city made of gold
And saved from the fire, yes, then I was sold!

Day 3: Tuesday

Out of Time, Out of Money, Out of Commission

Once in a while a movie comes along that is a witness to the plan of salvation and Yahweh's (God's) way of doing things all by itself. I watched the trailer for the new movie, _In Time_, starring Justin Timberlake where Time is the new currency. Okay, for the record, this concept is not new, but it really makes you sit back and think about how we waste our time. Of course, business people have always declared that "Time is money." We tell people "you waste my time, you waste my money." We want to get paid for our time, whether it's hourly, weekly or bi-weekly. We tell people we don't have time to spend doing such and such. Finally, we tell people that "my time is my time."

In the Timberlake movie, you don't age and you only get 25 years to live. Can you believe it, 25 years? Some of us have underwear older than that. One thing I notice in this movie is that you don't really have a choice when you reach 25. It doesn't matter whether or not you're sick or healthy. You will die. It is against the law for you to go beyond your 25 years.

So, okay, this movie does not really set a precedent. There was a 1976 movie that those of us older than 25 may remember. It was called _Logan's Run_ starring Michael York. Except in _Logan's Run_ you did age, but at least you had until the age of 30. When you turned 30, you had to die. So Logan and a female friend (character played by Jenny Agutter) managed to escape to Sanctuary. Yes, folks, it's the Adam and Eve and the search for the Garden of Eden (Utopia) all over again. However, at least the Creator gave man close to 1,000 years back in <u>Methuselah's</u> day. As time progressed, man's days got shorter and shorter. Of course, you only buy this if you believe what the <u>Bible</u> says, and I do.

However, there is <u>scripture</u> that says man is lucky to have lived 70 years, which is about average today. Even if we discard all of the forces against us in our struggle to survive each day – and we chuck *Logan's Run* and *In Time* into that abyss of make-believe because they are, after all, just sci-fi movies – we still come to the realization that 70 years is really not a long time, especially when compared to eternity.

Let's break it down into more bite-size reality. The <u>average heart rate</u> is about 72 bpm (beats per minute). During that minute, your heart pumps 2.5 liters of blood throughout your entire body. That's a lot of work for that little muscle, but it can take it – for a time anyway. People have been known to slow down their heart rate. For example, cyclists <u>Lance Armstrong</u> and <u>Miguel Indurain</u> were known to have heart rates as low as 32 and 28 bpm, respectively. If you can slow down your heart rate, it is possible to extend your life. That is, if you're not the characters portrayed by Michael York (*Logan's Run*) and Justin Timberlake (*In Time*).

So, if we use 70 as the average, you start off with 3,680 fun-filled weekends to find a "party over here" and a "party over there." Oh, but wait you've just been born. So, let's speed fast to the good time age of 20. By this time, you have 2,640 weekends left. At age 30, you have 2,120 weekends left. Over 1,500 weekends gone and you're just in your prime and just getting started. However, unlike the characters in the movie *In Time*, you are going to age. So, let's speed to age 40. By now, you have 1,600 weekends left. You've spent 2,000 weekends. Now you know why some claim life after 40 is over the hill (or downhill). By age 50, you're slowing down, your hair is greyer, and you have 980 weekends left. By the time you reach <u>legal retirement age</u>, you only have **416 weekends left**.

This is a time when most people only receive enough social security on which to survive until they die. Of course, there are those who manage to become wealthy along the way. However, they realize they've spent the majority of their lives losing their health trying to get wealthy, and now, lucky for the doctors and pharmaceutical companies, they will spend the last part of their lives losing their wealth trying to get healthy again.

Even if we live longer than 70 as some do, it's still not enough. In time, we will eventually run out of time. There's nowhere for us to run to find "sanctuary" on this planet or any other. The reality is that there is no guarantee most of us will make it to age 70, and, believe it or not, this world is not long to be here – that is, like I said, if you believe the Bible – and I do.

Day 3 S.O.S. Words of Inspiration

Instead of a poem, here are some last words of famous people who either knew or were unaware they were out of time:

Elizabeth I: "All my possessions for one moment of time."

Bing Crosby: "That was a great game of golf."

James Dean: "My fun days are over."

Mahatma Gandhi: "I am late by ten minutes. I hate being late. I like to be at the prayer punctually at the stroke of five."

Benjamin Franklin: "A dying man can do nothing easy."

Oscar Wilde: "My wallpaper and I are fighting a duel to the death. One or the other of us has to go."

Cardinal Borgia: "I have provided in the course of my life for everything except death, and now, alas, I am to die unprepared."

W.C. Fields: "I'm looking for a loophole."

Ludwid van Beethoven: "Too bad, too bad! It's too late!"

Sigmund Freud: "The meager satisfaction that man can extract from reality leaves him starving."

Socrates: "All of the wisdom of this world is but a tiny raft upon which we must set sail when we leave this earth. If only there was a firmer foundation upon which to sail, perhaps some divine word."

Phillip III, King of France: "What an account I shall have to give to God! How I should like to live otherwise than I have lived."

Jonathan Edwards: "Trust in God and you shall have nothing to fear."

D.L. Moody: "I see earth receding; heaven is opening. God is calling me."

Lew Wallace (author of *Ben Hur*): "Thy will be done."

Martin Luther: "Into Thy hands I commend my spirit! Thou hast redeemed me, O God of truth."

David Livingstone: "Build me a hut to die in. I am going home.

Day 4: Wednesday

P-E-R-F-E-C-T: Yes, That's What It Means To Me

What does it take to be perfect? I remember the movie from the 1979 Blockbuster movie "10," starring Bo Derek, child bride of "ancient of days" producer, John Derek, who was 30 years her senior. Supposedly, Ms. Derek became the standard of physical beauty for every woman. She was, in essence, considered "perfect" and sported a brand "new" hairstyle called "French Braids," you know much like the "Cornrows" that women of African descent had been wearing for thousands of years. And this, ladies and gentleman, without Ms. Derek having uttered one single solitary word – which, by the way, is the fantasy of most men.

Perfection for the male, on the other hand, was judged by a different standard. Most women, when asked who or what embodied the "perfect guy," would reply with a list of attributes that sounded more like a tall, dark and handsome St. Bernard than a real man.

Today, the standards have included certain factors such as dateability, intelligence, and whether his or her PhD also comes with a solid JoB. Of course, appearance is still a major factor and men remain "visual" while women remain "whishual." Yes, we are forever seeking perfection in each other while the divorce rate in the U.S. is at 50%. Well, so much for perfection.

If this futile search causes us to throw out the baby with the bathwater, there would be no one with whom we could talk or share or inevitably drive crazy. So, here we are with all of our naked imperfections trying to do as we've been instructed, "Be ye therefore perfect even as your Father which is in heaven is perfect" (Matthew 5:48). What was he thinking?! If you look in the dictionary under "imperfect" the chances are you'll see my picture. So, can we really reach perfection?

Well, let's take a look at what Yahoshua (Jesus) was really talking about. We have to go up a few scriptures in Matthew, Chapter 5, to get a better idea since Verse 48 culminates with a "therefore." When we examine Verses 43 through 47, we see that our Savior is telling us to love our enemies. Yes, we must love those creatures who despise us, who use us, who persecute us, who lie to us, who cheat on us, who disrespect us, who we'd like to take by the neck and . . . sorry, got carried away there. OK, I'm back.

So, why are we to do good to these loveable little enemies? He says because our Father in heaven "causes the sun to rise on the evil and the good, and sends rain on the righteous and the unrighteous" and what good is it "if you love those who love you, what reward do you have? Even the tax collectors do the same, don't they?" (Verses 45-46). Now hold on, tax collectors? They were considered sinners in Yahoshua's day, much like today.

But wait – sinners? Hey, that's us! Thank the Lord that "love shall cover the multitude of sins" (1 Peter 4:8). Finally, the apostle Sha'ul (Paul) reiterated what Yahoshua said. That's so Hebrew of him. After sending his second letter to soften his first letter of chastisement to the church in Corinth, he encouraged us to "be perfect, be of good comfort, be of one mind, live in peace; and the God of love and peace shall be with you" (2 Corinthians 13:11). Don't you just love him? He's one of my favorite OWIAC's.

Day 4 S.O.S. Words of Inspiration

Aretha wanted respect, but I want to be perfect
What it takes to get there, is it really worth it?

Can't be physically fit with my sedentary ways
So I'll strive for the spiritual and see how far it plays

My Savior wants me to love those that I'd like to hurt
And do good to them and even give them my shirt

So I'll give it a try, and just maybe by and by
This saved by grace sinner will come out a winner

Day 5: Thursday

We Don't Have to Sin

I'm sure none of us start off the morning by saying, "I think I'll commit a few sins today." That is, unless, God forbid, you're a homicidal maniac. If you're reading this, chances are you're not. If you are a serial killer, keep reading. In fact, go over to the right and read the previous devotionals also. Today is your day of deliverance.

I heard of someone whose prayer was: "Lord, thank you for waking me up today. I'm so glad that I haven't lied to anyone, that I haven't hurt anyone, that I haven't cursed anyone or given them the finger, that I haven't yelled at my family, that I haven't drank to excess, and haven't done anything wrong. But Lord, I'm going to get out of bed now, and I'm going to need your help the rest of the day."

Sound familiar? Well, when you need help, there's nothing wrong with asking for it. Sometimes just a simple prayer is enough to get the attention of our Creator in Heaven. "Unto you, O Lord, do I lift up my soul. O my God, I trust in you; let me not be ashamed, let not my enemies triumph over me." (Psalm 25:1-2) That was one of David's prayers. He exemplified the character of an OWIAC at its best. He broke every one of the Ten Commandments without breaking a sweat. He also knew how to repent. However, he didn't have to sin.

We don't have to sin. The trick is to learn, recognize, and avoid the enemy's traps, pitfalls, and little devices he uses against us. Remember, as Sha'ul (the apostle Paul) reminds us, "And no marvel; for Satan himself is transformed into an angel of light" (2 Corinthians 11:14). This is one of the enemy's devices. He deceives you by his physical appearance. If you haven't learned or are aware that demons as well as angels walk the earth, that they look like us, talk like us, and act like us, then you'd better delve into the scriptures just a bit more. I know you've been told that the "purpose of cloning research is to change living organisms so as to improve people's lives." Of course, cloning doesn't end with animals – it has and will continue with people. There are many people who support cloning for various reasons. I won't deal with this issue in depth here. I will only deal with the spiritual implications.

Cloned people and demons do not have the spirit of our Father who breathed into Adam. Demons carry the devil's spirit and they live here with us; however, they have no affect on you unless you desire them to do so. We've been given every protection we need. On a daily basis, we need to commit scripture to memory and it should be part of our minimal daily requirement just like vitamins for our physical health. Someone wrote a book that includes a "30-for-30" plan whereby you can assess your spiritual health, diagnose it, and apply specific healing from the Word. If you never know what state of spiritual health you're in, how will you know when you are most vulnerable and how to prevent yourself from getting sicker and sicker (continually sinning)?

The devil will attack you when you are at your most vulnerable point. Case in point, he did this to Yahoshua (Jesus) after he had fasted 40 days. Aha, his flesh was weak but spiritually he was strong. At each temptation, he counteracted with the Word. The important point is that each day of his life before he got to this point, he studied the Word which was what we know to be the Old Testament. It was he who inspired these words: "Thy word have I hid in mine heart, that I might not sin against thee." (Psalm 119:11)

The devil will even give you a flash intro of coming attractions to sin. He'll show you pictures of you enjoying and reveling in your past sins. He'll whisper enticing words to make it seem oh so appealing. It is at that time, you must remember that the apostle Peter warned us to "Be sober, be vigilant; because your adversary the devil, as a roaring lion, walketh about, seeking whom he may devour" (1 Peter 5:8). The devil is seeking to devour you. Therefore, you have to meet his lies and deceptions with scripture. Sometimes you have to run like Joseph did from Potiphar's wife. No, don't have an "innocent" lunch alone with a woman who is not your wife. No, don't allow a man who is not your husband to gently massage your shoulders because he claims to be an "expert" and does this as a sideline.

Seems old fashioned? Of course, it is. Today, a great deal of people dance to a different tune called "Defense Straddle Shuffle." Here's how the dance goes: you put your legs apart and bend slightly as if you're sitting on a fence. You take one step to the right and two steps to the left, now raise your arms in the air, and shake your body like you just don't care, and then dance yourself silly into sin.

We live in an age where just about anything goes, and the defense, or rather the excuse, people give is "It's all good." But we know it's not all good. Some things, especially sin, hurt us and everyone in our lives – those we know and those we don't know. Our brother, the apostle Paul said that, "If they shall fall away, to renew them again unto repentance; seeing they crucify to themselves the Son of God afresh, and put him to an open shame" (Hebrews 6:6). Everything we do affects someone or something. We don't live in a vacuum. Our Father knew what he was doing.

So, we really don't have to sin if we don't want to. However, it's not easy and it takes real Work and real Word. Just like anything else: no pain, no gain. From most things we can walk away; from others we may have to run. However, we can focus on and remember something our Savior said: "The thief cometh not, but for to steal, and to kill, and to destroy: I am come that they might have life, and that they might have it more abundantly." (John 10:10)

Day 5 S.O.S. Words of Inspiration

I can surely recognize the enemy's devices
They usually come during one of my crises

So, I'll arm myself with prayer and the Word
And let the devil know his schemes are absurd

For an OWIAC I am, but I don't have to sin
Just know my boundaries and to skillfully say "when"

Day 6: Friday

Deliver Us from Satan's 3 x's

The things I want to do; I don't. The things I don't want to do. Those things I do. Who will deliver me from this body of death?! The apostle Paul first spoke these words. I live them almost every day.

We all have our own individual faults and sins with which to contend. Pornography is mine. What's yours? At times you want to make yourself believe that because you're just watching and not committing the act as are the people in the video, that somehow you're not as guilty. But there is no big or little sin; there is just sin.

Our Savior said, "That whosoever looketh on a woman [or man] to lust after her hath committed adultery with her already in his heart." (Matthew 5:28). This goes for men and women. So we voyeurs are not excused and are all the more guilty. If you watch someone being killed (whether you are seen or not) and you silently revel in it, you are nonetheless an accessory to murder. It is as if you committed the act yourself.

Sometimes it feels as though we are living in the days of Sodom and Gomorrah. Sexual immorality of all kinds is rampant, and readily accessible for you to watch on the Internet. I researched some of the pornography statistics. It seems that every *second* over $3,000 is spent on pornography, with over 28,000 viewers over the Internet, and close to 400 users are typing adult search terms into search engines. Every **second**! That's not all, every 39 minutes a new porn video is being created in the United

States. So, you'd think the U.S. would be the money-making leaders in this venue. No, of course the leaders are China ($27.4 billion), South Korea ($25.7 billion), and Japan ($19.9 billion). The U.S. trails with $13.3 billion. How can we find billions to spend on this when 50% are out of work?! And these statistics are from 6 years ago.

Anyway you slice it, this sin of choice is big business and more of us are sucked into it every day. Close to 15% of all websites are from this industry. This amounts to 4.2 million sites with close to 500 **million** web pages. It gets worse. There are almost 70 million **daily** search engine requests for porn. There are about 2.5 billion pornographic emails sent out each day. Apparently, there are 100,000 websites offering child pornography. I've never seen any of them. I would say at least I'm not a pedophile and don't watch this type of porn; however, it doesn't matter. It's like someone saying they rob convenience stores but not banks, or that they rape prostitutes but not nuns, or that they sell drugs to strangers but not to friends and family, or that they murder ex-convicts but not law-abiding citizens. No big or little sin; just sin.

Although I've always known this industry is demonic and is condoned and operated by "spiritual wickedness in high places" (Ephesians 6:12b), it was not until recently that I realized just how evil the whole industry is. They pull you in just like drug dealers. They give you free samples and let you try it. The sites will let you view it for free. Most people are sucked into it to the point where they do spend money on it. Unfortunately for them, I do not and have not. Unfortunately for me, I pay with my time and leave my salvation in jeopardy – the biggest cost of all.

Sure, I can repent and do; however, repentance means to turn away from your sin, not back to it. I learned that all I had to do to access this vomit was to type into the search engine a little "x" three times. How appropriate that 3 x's and a blaring sound will signal a loss for one family on the Family Feud and win for those without the 3 x's. How appropraite that 3 x's signals three times you're out. However, through prayer I realized that Satan's realm, these 3 x's mean more than that.

Let me explain. Numerology plays a bigger part in our lives than we know. Never mind all of the spiritualists' mumbo-jumbo about the number '6' being "the most loving of all numbers." Our standard is the Bible. The letter 'x' is the 24th letter of the alphabet. If we add these numbers we get the number '6.' Repeated 3 times in succession, we get '666.' Messiah Yahoshua reveals to the apostle John and says, "Here is wisdom. Let him that hath understanding count the number of the beast: for it is the number of a man; and his number is Six hundred threescore and six" (Revelation 13:18). Remember, the devil can appear as an "angel of light" (2 Corinthians 11:14). So, it sounds highly likely that people will be deceived by numerologists and spiritualists who will claim the number of his name is a loving savior. However, this person is the beast of which the scriptures speak, and is, my friends, the anti-Messiah.

This spirit pervades every arena in which we live. Pornography is just one of them. Corruption is in education, sports, politics, religion, judicial system, government, and economics. Have I missed anything? I remember a few years ago how a petition with close to 300,000 signatures to remove 20 evangelists from the Internet. It matters not whether I agree with them or not. My concern is that the freedom of religious expression is always under attack. However, where are the petitions to remove porn from the Internet?! Where are the outcries against this medium being used for such degradation and spirit-debilitating activities?!

There are none. There will never be. My quest, as your quest, is to put on the whole armor of the Father to protect ourselves. We have a choice and we can choose not to partake of this arena. Despite the lure of this "drug," we must remember that we can do all things through Messiah Yahoshua who strengthens us (Philippians 4:13). Therefore, we can say NO. Here is some help from Psalm 38 written by our brother, David, to get Yah's attention:

Day 6 S.O.S. Words of Inspiration

1 O LORD, do not continue to rebuke me in your anger!
    Do not continue to punish me in your raging fury!
    2 For your arrows pierce me, and your hand
        presses me down.
    3 My whole body is sick because of your judgment;
        I am deprived of health because of my sin.
    4 For my sins overwhelm me; like a heavy load,
        they are too much for me to bear.
    5 My wounds are infected and starting to smell,
        because of my foolish sins.
    6 I am dazed and completely humiliated; all day long I
        walk around mourning.
    7 For I am overcome with shame and my whole body is
        sick.
    8 I am numb with pain and severely battered; I groan
        loudly because of the anxiety I feel.
    9 O Lord, you understand my heart's desire;
        my groaning is not hidden from you.
    10 My heart beats quickly; my strength leaves me; I can
        hardly see.
    11 Because of my condition, even my friends and
    acquaintances keep their distance; my neighbors
        stand far away.
    12 Those who seek my life try to entrap me; those who
        want to harm me speak destructive words;
        all day long they say deceitful things.
    13 But I am like a deaf man – I hear nothing; I am like a
        mute who cannot speak.
    14 I am like a man who cannot hear and is incapable of
        arguing his defense.
    15 Yet I wait for you, O LORD! You will respond, O Lord,

my God!

16 I have prayed for deliverance, because otherwise they
will gloat over me; when my foot slips they will
arrogantly taunt me.

17 For I am about to stumble, and I am in constant pain.

18 Yes, I confess my wrongdoing, and I am concerned
about my sins.

19 But those who are my enemies for no reason are
numerous; those who hate me without
cause outnumber me.

20 They repay me evil for the good I have done; though I
have tried to do good to them,
they hurl accusations at me.

21 Do not abandon me, O LORD! My God, do not remain far
away from me!

22 Hurry and help me, O Lord, my deliverer!

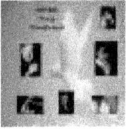

Day 7: Saturday

Is it a Sin to be Wealthy?

People are <u>starving</u> all over the world. In fact, almost 800 million people suffer from hunger. Every 3.6 seconds someone dies of hunger and every year 15 million children die of hunger. These statistics are startling in a world where there is so much abundance. However, the majority of the wealthy resides with the few compared to the masses. One third of the world is well-fed, one third is under-fed, and the last third is starving.

I am amazed every time I read articles about the rich and famous. Of course, not everyone who is rich is famous and not everyone who is famous is rich. I read stories about celebrities such as <u>Oprah</u>, who is worth a few billion dollars, <u>Jerry Seinfeld</u> who not only has close to a billion dollars, but he collects cars and houses all of them within a 4-story car garage. Anyone who has tried to find a parking space at an event and had to drive up two or three levels knows the multitude of cars this entails. Of course, this would mean he has to either pay people to service and take care of these cars for him or he has to spend time doing it himself, which, even if it's a hobby, is highly unlikely.

I hear stories of people winning close to $300 million dollars in the <u>lottery</u>, sometimes because they happen to buy a ticket by accident. What's even more appalling is when I learn that a lot of these people are not only broke or nearly broke within a few years, but they describe how the money was a "burden" or detail the troubles they encountered. I heard of a woman who had struggled raising her two children by herself and had to declare <u>bankruptcy</u>. She was now employed with a correctional facility where she's had feces thrown into her face by some of the inmates. She meant to buy one of the regular lottery tickets as she said she does every six months. However, she accidentally bought a Mega Million Lottery Ticket – and won $40 million dollars. Okay, so the good old IRS, a non-government, unconstitutional, for-profit entity, claims $10 million of this in taxes. What was even more amazing was that she said she didn't know what to do with that much money and she will not quit her job because her employers have been so good to her.

Since the beginning of time and throughout history, we hear of those who have killed and pillaged to control and claim territory. In other words, they took what they wanted and if others wanted to do the same, usually they were killed. This goes on even to this day. Once they controlled all of the resources they set up government and laws to make sure no one else would be able to do what they did. This is how they controlled the masses. Others who would need what the dictators had stolen would now have to work to get worthless pieces of paper (currency) to purchase what Yahweh (God) had already given to man freely: food, water, shelter, and land.

None of the governments have worked because none of them are what Yah intended. Capitalism, Communism, and Socialism are all different sides of the same coin. There is, even today, enough land and resources for everyone, yes, for all 7 billion people in the world. So why are people starving? Because of greed and selfishness.

Everything that Yahoshua (Jesus) warned us about: the lust of the flesh, the lust of the eye, and the pride of life, are the very evils that have crushed our earthly economy and left us spiritually bankrupt. Jesus had to fast 40 days and 40 nights to be strengthened against these same temptations. He was tested and tried and emerged victoriously. (Matthew 4:1-11) The spirits of greed and selfishness are concoctions from the devil himself. He, once called Lucifer, the bright and morning star, rebelled against a holy and just Creator. Lucifer was cast down along with a third of the fallen angels. It is they who control this world and its evil and unjust system. This spirit has pervaded every facet. The spirit of Anti-Messiah (Antichrist) has darkened the minds of so many. Human life is worth nothing to them. Their consciences have been seared and they have been blinded with the quest for what they believe is success, fame, glory, and wealth. They know that "he who controls the gold controls the world," and they are intent on doing just that: controlling the world. There is no compassion in their hearts for others. In fact, some of them delight in knowing that they have taken away everything from others and they, they alone, are without equal monetarily. They are like little boys struggling, fighting, and killing to come away with all of the marbles in their bags.

Yahoshua says we live in this world but we are not of this world. He reminds us not to worry about anything, but to take one day at a time. People who amass more than they could possibly use in one lifetime claim they are doing so to leave a legacy and to build security for their children and their children. However, wise Solomon, a man of Yah without equal in wealth, warned us that it is all "vanity," which translated means "nothingness." Most people with extreme wealth are so consumed with trying to make more money and finding ways to protect their wealth, they don't really take time to enjoy their lives. I used to envy them; now I pity them. I am reminded of the story of the rich young ruler whose sole goal in life was to build additional facilities to house his assets. We can liken this to the filthy rich who have countless Swiss and offshore bank accounts containing dollar amounts that would seem unreal to most of us. The same thing Yah said to the rich man in the Bible story is the same thing Yah says to the wealthy today: "You fool, this night your soul is required." (Luke 12:20).

Day 7 S.O.S. Words of Inspiration

How can I turn by back on those with no food?
How can I be so selfish and so utterly crude?

In a world of capitalism it is still just greed
On the backs of the under-class I happy feed

I know for everyone there is surely enough
But to give up what I have is way too tough

So out of my abundance I'll share my bankroll
For in so doing, I will deliver my soul

"Then Jesus beholding him loved him, and said unto him, *One thing thou lackest: go thy way, sell whatsoever thou hast, and give to the poor, and thou shalt have treasure in heaven: and come, take up the cross, and follow me."* **(Mark 10:21)**

Last Words of Encouragement

My Dear Fellow OWIAC:

Hopefully, after these 7 days, you have realized that Messiah Yahoshua (Jesus Christ), soon to return, is the answer to every one of your problems and indiscretions.

May you find peace and forgiveness in the bosom of our Savior who said to the woman caught in adultery (sinner):

"Where are your accusers? ... Neither do I condemn you; go and sin no more."

(See John 1-11)

About The Author

Dr. Elizabeth A. James (E.A. James) has been writing for over 40 years. She is a licensed and ordained minister and has been President and Founder of Fast And Indispensable Temporary Help (F.A.I.T.H.) Ministries, Inc. since February, 1999. She is also the Editor-in-Chief of FM Publishing Company (2009) and Senior Managing Director of Geri Lorraine Enterprises, LLC (2000). In 2014, she became a supplier, independent marketer, and supporter with TAG Team Marketing International and a dedicated member of the Black Business Network.

After attending over 10 colleges, she has a doctorate in Theology & Biblical Counseling, a master's in Education, bachelor's degree in English, and major course work in subjects such as Business Management, Biomedical Engineering, Pre-Med, and Chemistry.

In addition to many other accomplishments, E.A. James has received the Woman of Excellence Award, is a member of blackwritersconnect.com, and has won several awards for her poetry. She is currently a business consultant, certified teacher, and a Nationally-Certified Manager of Program Improvement.

Titles by E.A. James:

Spiritual Cosmetics for the Soul (devotionals)
The Last Visitor (historical fiction)
Being a Well Body of Believers (nonfiction)
This Hill I Climb (poetry)
The Reason Why I Sing (poetry/songs)
Driving Tips for BOOHs (Bats Out of Hell) (satire)
7-Day Emergency Help for OWIACs (Of Whom I Am Chief) (devotionals)
Why I Should Hate Men, But Don't (nonfiction)
Will Work for Food, Family & Freedom (nonfiction)
Casino Con: An Eye-Opening Look From the Inside Out (nonfiction)

Book Ordering Information

To order other books by E.A. James or books published by FM Publishing Company, or to inquire about screenplay production rights, go to:

www.fmpublishingcompany.com

www.blackbusinessnetwork.com/doctorlj

www.createspace.com

www.amazon.com

www.lightningsource.com

Email: fmpublishing@cox.net

Fax: 800-518-1219

www.ingramcontent.com/pod-product-compliance
Lightning Source LLC
Chambersburg PA
CBHW060547030426
42337CB00021B/4466